*Crown Your Shame*

AF080559

## OrangeBooks Publication

1st Floor, Rajhans Arcade, Mall Road, Kohka, Bhilai, Chhattisgarh 490020

Website:**www.orangebooks.in**

### © Copyright, 2024, Author

Scripture quotation marked (KJV) are from the King James Version and are in the Public domain

Scripture quotation marked (NLT) are from copyright© 1996, 2004, 2015 by Tyndale Charitable Trust.

Scripture quotation marked (NIV) are taken from the Holy Bible, New International Version®, NIV®. Copyright© 1973, 1978, 1984, 2011 by Biblica, Inc. ™ Used by permission of Zondervan. All rights reserved worldwide. Www.zondervan.com The "NIV" and "New International Version" are trademarks registered in the United States Patent and Trademark Office by Biblica, Inc. ™

All emphases within scriptural quotations are the author's own.

All rights reserved. No part of this book may be reproduced or transmitted in any form or by any means, electronic or mechanical, including photocopying, recording, or by any information storage and retrieval system, without permission in writing from the author.

### First Edition, 2024

**ISBN:** 978-93-6554-503-6

# CROWN
## —YOUR—
# SHAME

## KANI DAVID T

OrangeBooks Publication
www.orangebooks.in

# Dedication

This Book is Dedicated to

God the Father, God the Son, and God the Holy Spirit.

Without you Guys, none of this would have been possible!

# Introduction

A love book from the Heavenly Father to the Fatherless Children, broken homes, betrayed hearts, abused and neglected ones, overlooked and bullied, single-parent, divorced and barren woman. You are the most POWERFUL warriors that the world can contain. The battles and attacks of your life was not for everyone because there's so much TREASURE and VALUE within you. You are a threat to the kingdom of darkness and that's the primary reason you were challenged the entire life. Not anymore! Take Courage today, as you read now, I pray that you will have a strong encounter with our Lord Jesus. God wants you to take each and every lines written in this book to be yours personally. He counts you as His most precious and priceless possession.

Every contents in the book is from a real battle where God has encountered the person to overcome the challenges that came in life. Just believe the Lord is speaking and you will start hearing His voice from now, He is not a God of partialities, His royal position of being the King of Kings and the Lord of Lords doesn't disqualify you out of His sight. Although He is Royal and Rich, He takes pleasure to be a Father to Fatherless, a Hero to the broken hearts, a Husband to widows and separated ones.

This book will lead you to know who you are and it will be a great weapon to dismantle yourself from all the pain, shame, failures, cheap names which were called out, the emotional traumas, betrayals and the pasts.

Time to unlock the REAL YOU, get ready to walk in Boldness by shining out of your Shame and enjoy your Crown.

Read every scriptures mentioned in the book, as it is the very breath that will impact you to be transformed. His breath is life and it is waiting to pour out the streams of living water into your new life.

Your season is about to change from now in the name of Jesus. Everything that was keeping you in bondage is being broken now with the blood of Jesus. Expect a massive transformation to quickly happen over your life.

# Testimony

This book is a testimony of a little girl who has escaped hell with the power of knowing her true IDENTITY. It's the encounter between JESUS and this girl that transformed her life completely. The girl in the story is myself and I'm praying this will inspire and build every readers to discover your real identity in CHRIST.

I was born and raised in a slum which is situated in the city of Bangalore, India. We were 4 in number as a family, Father, Mother and an elder sister. As a growing child, all I ever experienced was shame, guilt, disaster, pain, abuse, betrayal and mental trauma. It was hard for me to receive and experience a family love. Loneliness and isolation was rooted right from a tender age as I never had any earthly father's affection. My mother was abandoned with two little girls in her responsibility, life wasn't fair unless she decided to work and sacrifice her earnings on us. My Father was a prayerful man and ministering but lost his spirituality as soon as I was born into the family. He preferred a boy child and I turned out to be a girl.

He became mentally sick, abusive, drunkard and stopped taking care of the family. On the other hand, my mother took the hardship of bringing us up in a Metro City by educating us in a good school. Although my mother took me to church, the chaos and the difficulties blinded my eyes and the enemy took advantage of this and kept me away from receiving a lot of spiritual blessings and gifts in my early age.

In search of Love, I got betrayed with a relationship during my teen ages, this caused me to hate Men and marriage. Not every people liked or accepted our family with kindness and love even though they were Christians. The society labelled us as outcasts and I strongly fed myself to be a curse.

However, My creator never saw my family in such manner and His hands of guidance and protection was around us every time. It was through God's pure grace that I completed my education and It was God my Father who has placed me into good positions in the workplace. My Lord was and is faithful till today, though I was failing Him due to sin and spiritual blindness, He never left me away. My faith was challenged since childhood with struggles and emotional hurts. Yet, my heart was always encouraged to find strength in His Word and Presence.

One fine day, My father went missing as he was mentally ill, we searched him everywhere and couldn't find him, this caused my mother to have the same mental sickness too. It was a hard time for us to find peace as we had to admit her in the hospital. The Lord showed up supernaturally and helped us to treat her by sending the right people to help. This moment is truly to be witnessed for His glory. My Mother moved to hometown Kanyakumari, Tamil Nadu - South India and got settled in the same place. I was left alone in the city for around 4 years. There was emptiness within me and my soul was filled with pain, this situation made me an insecure person which made me loos hopes on family and marriage. But, the search of affection never stopped and I was confused, got trapped into the same gender relationship. My life was such a mess that the enemy took advantage of this sin to push me into this dangerous trap of driving me to hell. However, the compassion of my Heavenly Father never left me, the precious Holy Spirit convicted me of my sin and led me to a different church through one of my friends in Christ.

Watching an abusive marriage within family is the hardest thing any child can undergo, I had no hopes towards any relationships but the LORD comforted me every time I spent time with Him in prayer and worship. Anytime I hear the word "FATHER" in sermons, my heart would be filled with the mighty presence of the LORD and tears would roll down immediately. It was the depth of His Pure Love, which made me seek Him for a marriage in prayers and worship. Precious Holy Spirit is truly a divine help for every believer in Christ, He's a real person who tries to search us to convey the compassion that the LORD wants to offer every sinners. Even during my days of unbelief, the Holy Spirit encouraged me to pray and take counsel from the LORD to have hopes on marriage and a future family. After praying for a couple of years, when I was loosing my faith, the LORD led me to my partner who was divorced, yet serving the Lord faithfully. Holy Spirit empowered me to pray about the situation and I continued to pray. As we continued praying, the Lord helped me to approach my home with the proposal, there was perfect peace and I knew it was the Lord's will. We are happily married today, serving the Lord together by accepting each other in a new way, having the lens of Jesus. Truly the Lord has fulfilled my heart's desire.

Here I am testifying today through this book for a successive marriage, forgiveness of sins and a complete restoration from my past traumas and pain. LORD JESUS is truly a genuine lover of your soul, and He will never stop you or treat you with discouragements for your pasts, sin, shame or dirty backgrounds. You are His Jewell and His treasure that He gave His very own life in order to own you. I thank God for His faithful hands over my life which has made me an over comer till this day. Our God is truly faithful and He isn't done with us unless we reach and inherit His promises.

I believe this book inspires you to find the power within yourself which is a weapon from our Heavenly Father above, it is a gift rooted in each one of us to overcome the demonic agendas from Hell. Yes, it is possible to stamp and destroy the evil schemes designed by the enemy, as we are the rightful sons and daughters of a great King who has purchased each and every flesh and bone walking on this planet with His ROYAL PURE BLOOD.

His blood is for every breath still alive, there is no favoritism in His eyes, all it requires is a believing heart to receive Him in whichever situation we are living. Hence Dare to Believe every promise written in this book is for you and your bright future.

I am asking and requesting the Lord for a complete restoration and transformation of your heart.

Be blessed and stay fruitful.

# Contents

1. You Are Owned ............................................................ 1
2. Know Your Power ........................................................ 6
3. Be Bold as a LION ...................................................... 11
4. Celebrate The Real You ............................................. 16
5. You are designed for greatness ................................ 21
6. Dare To Break the Stereotype .................................. 27
7. You are not a burden ................................................ 31
8. Conclusion ................................................................. 36
9. About Our Ministry ................................................... 38

# 1

## You Are Owned

# You Are Owned

A Father to the Fatherless - There is no creation on this planet earth without a owner. Know that you are owned by a Heavenly Father above. Every growing child yearns for a father's love and support during the life journey, not just a child, every human beings need this special love, comfort, support, affection until eternity and beyond. This is available with our Father who is generous in satisfying every living creation turning towards Him with a true heart and mind. Every pain filled situation in a human's life comes from a lack of understanding that we are alone, that is a lie, nobody is alone and we are owned by an eternal Father. Psalms 68:5 says, A Father to the Fatherless, and a judge of the widows, is God in His holy habitation. We are owned by our Father in heaven, not as strangers but as His own children. No matter the age or background, He celebrates in owning you. You are His precious Jewell. When the world names the people filled with troubles as outcasts, God wants to reveal Himself as a dear and loving Father to such outcasts in a solid way to show that He cares and He finds pleasure to own them as His Own son and daughter.

The primary fact that each and every individual must recognize is, "there is a devouring enemy assigned for each and every individual on this earth." However, the creator of heaven and the earth ELOHIM is a wonderful Hero who steps in to rescue every individuals from the enemy's trap. Our Father is a warrior and He is excellent in His strategies to empower us to defeat the power of the enemy over our lives. Exodus 15:3 says - The LORD is a man of war: the LORD is his name. Be aware that you are owned and sealed by a warrior around you throughout this life's journey. Silence every other negative voice in your mind and allow the Holy Spirit to fill you with this truth. Father in the heaven takes it as a prime responsibility to fulfill the needs of the abandoned, fatherless, widows the orphans.

Each and every eyes crossing over the name of Jesus is highly precious to Him. Even you, currently holding this book are dear and loving to Him. Psalms 37:23 - The steps of a good man are ordered by the Lord: and he delighteth in his way. He finds pleasure in each and every detail of your life.

The increase of responsibilities in our lives brings pressure and chaos along with anxiety as per the pattern of the world. However, it is time to realize that you are truly owned by a Heavenly Father who is capable of doing impossibilities in your life only if you can trust Him wholeheartedly. He finds it an opportunity to lift your burdens and to take care of your responsibilities as His own. Psalms 27:10 - Though my Father and Mother forsake me, the LORD will receive me. There are circumstances in my life, where I was abandoned and isolated with nobody to address my emotional traumas and needs but the true love of God has found me and searched me in various ways which is repeatedly proving till today that He owns everyone who believes His name. During childhood, I remember my school fees getting paid by a teacher, and there were a couple of lecturers who came forward to pay my college fees too. He is truly a Father to the Fatherless and He finds pleasure in helping the helpless and the needy. It was the favor of God on my life that moved people to give the help. Any moment you are discouraged by this society and the label the world throws on you, just kill those lies around and stand firm with the truth of your true identity - You are Owned forever by your Heavenly Father.

If the upbringing of our family is full of abuse, pain and childhood hurt, the world around will convince you to think bad about yourself, it will even make you look like you are cursed and aren't fit to belong to God's family. When the head of a family is a failure, you will always be forced to carry a signature as a son or daughter of a useless family as per the pattern of this world. Sadly, this pattern is still followed by many of the believers in Christ as well, but the one who truly owns you says, My thoughts are not your thoughts, neither are your ways my ways, declares the LORD in Isaiah 55:8. The way you think about yourself is important as you belong to the royal bloodline of the LORD. Once you are a born again believer, you no longer belong to the family bloodline of your earthly parents. Colossians 1:13 - For He has rescued us from the kingdom of darkness and transferred us to the kingdom of his beloved Son, You become a new Son and a Daughter in God's kingdom as the born again experience begins in your life. Which means, you now talk and walk like a King's daughter/Son, your thinking pattern becomes like the one who truly owns you as His own Child. Reject and kill every labels the society imposes on you and start seeing yourself as a Kingdom child because that is the truth about you.

Sometimes, due to the brokenness and the emptiness, we tend to follow the world, and the so called "depression" tends to make us fall into addictions such as alcohol, smoke, cinemas, porn and useless television shows stoping ourselves to search our Father in prayer and worship, by making us forcefully believe that we are outcasts, this traps our soul into the very darkness that the enemy uses to keep our minds locked into slavery. Everything the world offers to ease your mind is temporary and it will never satisfy your heart nor soul, the key to feel special and important is not found in friendships, relationships, family, best jobs, titles or status. It is found in Lord Jesus. The moment your heart realizes that you are accepted just the way you are with all the mess you've been through and there is a permanent eternal love on your side is the exact moment when your heart will truly be satisfied. Luke 23:43 - "Today, you will be with me in paradise." Our LORD doesn't look into our sins, He looks us with the eyes of compassion and He would love to Own each and every heart turning to Him. He waits for us to hold on to Him by forgetting the dirty pasts and sins. Just Hold onto Him and enjoy His Ownership on your life. Forget the pasts hurts, labels imposed by family, relatives and the wicked society. Embrace the love of the LORD today.

This book didn't come into your hands accidentally, you are His Special One, His Chosen One, His Anointed One, His Own Treasure You are.! Your past doesn't matter anymore and you are NEW completely from today and forever, Accept His Love today and declare the Ownership between the LORD and you with the below prayer by reading it aloud.

**PRAYER -** Heavenly Father, I come into your loving presence with the blood of LORD JESUS all over me, thank you for setting me free today from all of my pain in the pasts, sin, traumas, childhood abuse and hurts. I am no more the old me but the loving Son/Daughter of your kingdom. Thank you for giving me the sonship through LORD JESUS. I declare that

I am a new creation in CHRIST. I declare that I am accepted and free from sin. My past and sin shall no more have control over me. I am a child of God loved for who I am in CHRIST now and forever. Thank you for making me yours and owning me, I declare that I am OWNED by LORD JESUS. Amen!

# 2

## Know Your Power

# Know Your Power

There is a hidden power in our weakness, the foolish things of this world has the strength of God. Our God finds it interesting to bring beauty out of ashes. He is specialised in making the foolish things of this world to shame the wise. 1 Corinthians 1:27 - But God chose the foolish things of the world to shame the wise; God chose the weak things of the world to shame the strong. Your life might be a life filled with struggles, difficulties, shame, rejection, abuse and the world would have seen your circumstances as something that is too low or very foolish. But the truth is, there is a powerful story of yours which is hidden inside the shame, abuse and condemnation to serve as a medicine for the suffering and hurting souls with the similar situation. Come to a realisation that it is for God's glory your life is designed with so called foolish labels by the wicked society. Every dead situation in your life is a rescue mission for a bunch of crowd who is still stuck with the same pain. God never wastes any season of your lives, when the world mocks at your long time suffering as a curse, the LORD looks into your situation as He saw Joseph, David, Daniel, Esther, Ruth, Gideon and Jesus Himself. There is no leader without bloodshed and no champion without suffering. Every leader is trained and equipped hard and that is the reason your life is full of hardship.

There is power in suffering, get to a realisation of knowing the value in your pain. Not everyone is born to become a leader, but those who are qualified with certain discipline and hardship will become a leader. When you see your life as a problem, God sees a leader who is powerful in you. 1 Peter 2:9 - "But you are a chosen generation, a royal priesthood, a holy nation, His own special people, that you may proclaim the praises of Him who called you out of darkness into His marvelous light". The LORD qualifies people with a life of suffering to rule with Him in eternity, especially the ones who were filled with darkness in their lives are automatically chosen for His praises. It is a privilege to have hardships since childhood, stop seeing your life of mess as a curse, instead rejoice in the LORD for He has ordained and chosen you to live a life of royalty. Rejections from the world qualifies you to be a powerful vessel in the kingdom of God. Not just the life after eternity, but even during the journey on the earth you are born to be a leader. Do not waste your story but start executing every test into a testimony, every pain into a purpose.

You are powerful with dark pasts, the moment you come out of that darkness, your Father in heaven accepts you into His marvellous light which automatically makes you a priest to rule in His kingdom. Stop looking at your shame, guilt and condemnation and celebrate the kingship and the royalty that the LORD has provided for you.

Your power is in your own thinking. Your thoughts are what you become. Genesis 1:26 says, Then God said, "Let us make mankind in our image, in our likeness, so that they may rule over the fish in the sea and the birds in the sky, over the livestock and all the wild animals, and over all the creatures that move along the ground." You are created to dominate and rule this earth, that is in your DNA, and everything is supposed to be ruled by you.

This is your true POWER and it is hidden within your body. Whether a male or female, you are His child and you are supposed to see and operate in this world just like your Father in heaven. God doesn't rule and control us, He leads us into the right path, and so are you called to lead with your gifts and passions for His kingdom.

He is a God of heaven and earth, there is no battle which is lost by Him, it is His breath which is inside your lungs right now keeping the body alive, which means there is nothing dead in His breath, His breath produces life, It is a life giving breath. Genesis 2:7 - Then the LORD God formed the man from the dust of the ground. He breathed the breath of life into the man's nostrils, and the man became a living person. Come into an agreement of having the living power within yourself, unless you breath the last breath here on earth, the LORD is not done with you.

His breath is the power which makes the body to function, and you are walking, talking and living with the same breath even today, this shows you are powerful just like your Heavenly Father, if you begin to think just like Him, you can also bring the manifestations of heaven into your personal life. The moment you discover who you are, your thinking patterns will automatically sync with the Heavenly Father, it is because you truly belong to Him and you are a POWERFUL being just like Him.

When we think about the glory of God, it is huge and massive. There is no one like Him and no one will ever be. But what is that, He finds in us to take such a pleasure of. Psalm 8:4 - What is man that you are mindful of him, And the son of man that you care for him? Understand the power behind this words, The LORD GOD expects each of His children to be powerful just like Him. Along with His glorious existence, He constantly thinks about you every second and He is mindful of you. Judges 6:11 - 16, Here we see Gideon who is afraid of the enemies, and He has an encounter with the angel of the LORD.

When Gideon was asked to go and rescue Israel, his immediate response was "but how can I save Israel? My clan is the weakest in Manasseh, similarly today you might be feeling the weakest of all your family, friends, relatives, colleagues, church members and all your surroundings, Just know that, the LORD finds you as the perfect member to exhibit His mighty power through you. Our God is specialist in finding the least and the dust of this world to perform His mighty acts.

You might be comparing your life to high things of this world but those doesn't have the power which is within your weakness to bring down the glory of God into this earthly realm. Hence keep rejoicing the heaviness and the burdens in your life, though it might be frustrating at times, it will have its own way out with the help of God.

God calls you as a "Mighty Warrior" for enduring the hardship so far. As you endure the path of life with all the challenges on your way, you are not only becoming a champion on earth alone but a warrior in the spiritual realm as well. Kingdom of God is for warriors and not for easy goers. Every time you feel oppressed with the chaos and burdens which is dumped on your shoulder, hang on to God's words to bring you through.

The bonus for crossing over the pain and the suffering is, you are personally advancing in the kingdom as well.

Every great leaders in the book of the bible asked the LORD how can I? Why me? How can a foolish background as mine bring deliverance to people. I myself am a weak person. But God finds the useless, foolish and weakest mindset's as a POWERHOUSE to use them for His purposes on the earth. So, you see, you are the most eligible soldier to be a witness in the end times for His glory.

You are reading these lines not by an accident, it is the set time and the right season for you to know that "YOU ARE A MIGHTY WARRIOR" and the LORD celebrates your bravery. When rest of the world found the life's challenges as an obstacle, you overtook them and stood by faith to bring honor and glory to His name. Your hardships are not in vain, your difficult situations are not wasted, it is well noticed and you are gloriously triumphing over the challenges. Say aloud the prayer mentioned below and declare your victories ahead.

**PRAYER -** Heavenly Father, I come into your presence with the blood of Jesus all around me. Thank you for the strength and grace which you gave me until this day. May your power be revealed in me Lord, I celebrate every weakness in my life. Thank you for enlightening with your word of truth and I surrender my life in your loving hands to use me for your glory. I bless your name Lord. In Jesus name I pray. Amen.

# 3

# Be Bold as a LION

# Be Bold as a LION

Being Bold is your birthright, it's in your DNA to live a life of bravery. Proverbs 28:1 - The wicked flee though no one pursues, but the righteous are as bold as lion. You are righteous because of Lord Jesus! This is not something which you deserve, but it is a gift. His blood makes us righteous. Receive the righteousness with faith, by accepting His blood. 1 Corinthians 5:21 - God made him who had no sin to be sin for us, so that in him we might become the righteousness of God. So, you see, you are Righteous! It's time for you to be bold now. Every bleeding hearts since childhood is gifted with courage and the enemy knows about the power you carry, so he starts his schemes of destroying the boldness within you right from the childhood by silencing your voice, overlooking and oppressing as the least one in the world, so that you become the victim of insecurity, oppression, loneliness and all sort of unworthy feelings towards yourself. However, the fact is every shameful situation of your life was permitted for God's glory. God is not human, that he should lie, not a human being, that he should change his mind. Does he speak and then not act? Does he Promise and not fulfil - Numbers 23:19. The embarrassing moments are for your elevation and promotion alone.

Joseph was in the pit of shame and bullying without knowing the promotion ahead. David was not even considered when Samuel came to anoint him. Esther was an orphan, but God promoted her and trusted her boldness to subdue the enemy's power. When God has promised such a huge blessing for shame, then it's time for us to leave our ego and pride to humbly seek Him for the portion of blessings over our lives. Be brave enough to leave your backgrounds and get ready to walk into places with your heads high keeping this promise inside the heart. Every human that has caused shame into your life has provoked a huge blessing. Start thanking God for the humiliating situations as you are eligible and qualified for a massive promotion. Revelation 1:6 - He has made us a kingdom of priests for God his Father. All glory and power to him forever and ever! Amen. Trust this word with a courageous heart because you are born to serve a greater kingdom. You are purchased by the precious blood of Jesus, which means every shame, rejection and pain has lost its power because you are now in the Royal Bloodline of Jesus! Don't ever allow any demon to criticise you with these labels. Once you are fully convinced about this truth, a true Power and Boldness will arise within you. With this boldness you get the authority to be the kings and priests in our Lord's kingdom.

1 Peter 2:9 - But you are a chosen generation, a royal priesthood, a holy nation, His own special people, that you may proclaim the praises of Him who called you out of darkness into His marvelous light". God is not looking for people who were raised in a bright palace to be leaders in His kingdom, He is desperately looking for those who have faced the most dark situation with bravery of knowing and accepting Lord Jesus as their Savior, You are the champ who can be used to display the power of God. Get the courage to insert this truth within you that the shame in your life is for receiving a double portion of blessings. Start expecting the miracles right away and throw away every negative spirits speaking lies about your identity.

We live in a Voice activated Kingdom. John 1:1 - God made everything with word. The sound of our voice is powerful and it has the electricity to bring heaven down to earth. Just using your voice isn't enough, use it with an authority and a command which will bring a greater impact that can change lives and destinies. Proverbs 18:21 - Life and death are in the power of the tongue. Use your tongue wisely to be a blessing to your own life. I remember the days when people literally mocked at me saying, "Will anything good come out of her or Will She have a good Marriage".

Here I am testifying for the glory of king Jesus who has graced me with a dream marriage and a loving Husband who has given me the best days of my life. So, you see, there is power when you pray and use your tongue on your promises. You can design your own life into a blessing by the power of your Voice. What humans say as a curse, God can turn that into a blessing. I advise you to boldly approach the church places where you are locally situated to seek God's presence in prayer and worship. Don't be a silent member there but use your Voice, use it with authority and power for God to make a move in your life. Bold faith is honoured by God! He eagerly looks for His sons and daughters to come and speak to Him in boldness to smash and destroy all the garment of shame used by the enemy over our lives. You might be a single parent, divorced, broken in relationship or fatherless, here's the good news, our God is an expert in wiping away the shame with His blood. He's God of million chances and He expects your heart to be fully surrendered unto Him. Hebrews 4:16 - So let us come boldly to the throne of our gracious God. There we will receive his mercy, and we will find grace to help us when we need it most. Have the courage to search God in all situations, be bold to step into His presence even if you have messed up everything, because He can change your future forever with His blood.

Boldness brings you freedom and there's no other gift as walking in true liberty. Be free in knowing you are free from the names given by the society, accept your new identity in Christ and be bold in your thoughts and mind to show and project yourself as a free son and daughter filled with honor and riches in the kingdom, that is how God sees you. Jeremiah 31:3 - The love that God has on you is everlasting and it is beyond eternity, this love is not based on anything that you did to deserve, but it is due to His rich kindness. Every insecurity you see in yourself is dying today in Jesus name. This everlasting love is beside you despite the situations of your life. Romans 8:1 - So now there is no condemnation for those who belong to Christ Jesus. God has deposited his gifts in each of your lives which should be manifested for taking the gospel to the ends of the earth. This requires boldness, most of the lives filled with shame and condemnations leads to self doubt, unworthiness and low self esteem but these are the strategies of the enemies to stop you from using your gift even from the childhood. Everybody cannot be bold! Only those who have fought the toughest battles will stand to the ground with strength. So you see, you are automatically chosen and approved of God to take message of Christ to the world.

All you need is the testimony of your life, no seminars or special trainings are required to take Christ to the world.

Don't be ashamed of the Gospel, it is rewarding to work for the kingdom of God with our testimonies. Gospel is to be preached with power and boldness and that's possible with the Holy Spirit alone. For He is the precious Friend and our comforter who convicts us of our sins and He is the one who turns our hearts towards Jesus. You need his help to shine from your shame, Acts 1:8 - But you will receive power when the Holy Spirit comes on you; and you will be my witnesses in Jerusalem, and in all Judea and Samaria, and to the ends of the earth. Reserve this word as a treasure in your heart, you will start shining from your shame and your crown will literally be the brightest. Take away the shyness within you to shine. It is impossible to overcome the schemes of the enemy without testifying what God has done to you. Revelation 12:11 - And they overcame him by the blood of the Lamb, and by the word of their testimony; and they did not love their lives unto death. The enemy will be shamed when we unhide our shame to glorify God and testify about Lord Jesus. The moment you testify about Jesus, your boldness will increase and you will start walking with kingdom authority.

No devil can make you think less about yourself, it is important to testify with your mouth. God is counting on your life to reveal Himself to many others in similar situations. Your battles are not in vain, the life challenges, mockery, shame and abuse, rejection, sexual abuse has made you the bold person standing today to testify about the redeeming power of Lord Jesus. He has healed you and you are ready to bring others to Him. Start walking with boldness from this moment and say the prayer below aloud.

**PRAYER** - Father, I come into your presence with the precious blood of Jesus, and I thank you for talking to me. Lord May your glory be revealed through me, I pray for boldness upon me to testify your name to the ends of the earth. Thank you for removing the shameful thoughts from my mind, heart and spirit. I reject all the spirits of rejections and negativities by the power of your name Jesus. From today I am a living testimony and a walking miracle to glorify you everywhere that you place me Lord. Help me to live a life of surrender unto you Lord. In Jesus name I pray. Amen.

# 4

## Celebrate The Real You

# Celebrate The Real You

You are altogether beautiful My Darling, beautiful in every way - Song of Solomon 4:7. Yes, My reader of these lines, You are way too beautiful than words can describe in your own way. These words are my breath leading you to your actual IDENTITY which is in me says the LORD. Every other voices which has described you until now are lies and they are not My Voice. My sheep knows my voice and heeds to it. It's time to celebrate and dance with the Lord from now. No matter the age, size of your body, skin texture, length of the hair or your physical appearance, just remember this word which is the truth about you. You are beautiful just the way you are. Smile and never dim your light for anything in your life. Be totally comfortable to walk and talk the way you are originally designed. Don't consider the bullying comments you receive from family, toxic friends, social media. God's voice will never condemn and shame any one. His mind is full of us. Isaiah 55:8,9 - God's thoughts are high as the heavens and it is far better and even best to you. The difficult situations and the negativity around your life is not the reality, a shame filled life is not what the Father requires of us.

He sees each and every detail of you to be shining brightly because He created you with His very own hands and nothing that has happened to your life can stop the way He views his children and you are the child of the most High God. God your father is the only person cheering up and expecting you to wake up from that ashes and the lies of the enemy to shine for Him.

Isaiah 54:4,5 - Fear not, you will no longer live in shame. Don't be afraid; there is no more disgrace for you. You will no longer remember the shame of your youth and the sorrows of widowhood. For your Creator will be your husband; the LORD of Heaven's Armies is his name! He is your Redeemer, the Holy One of Israel, the God of all the earth. This word of life and truth is especially written from the breath of Yahweh to all the rejected and abandoned souls. The fatherless, divorced, widows and the rejected souls are loved by God.

And He takes them as His own. God is eager to see, if His children can bring the shame to His altar so that He can remove the disgrace from their lives, but due to ego, pride and humility issues we often miss the opportunity kept before us.

Practice and train your heart, soul and mind to seek God even if there is shame around, even if there is a crowd bullying you for your traumas and unfortunate situations, God stands as your bodyguard and He would personally defend you and cause others to move in love and respect towards you. Keep your intensions and thoughts high about yourself no matter what you've been through, have a strong mind and feed this truth within your heart because his thoughts are pure and genuine. This will only bless you and guard you from unwanted atmosphere.

His voice is the only truth you need, to be a thriving personality in this world. Everything else is falling apart. Mathew 24:35 - Heaven and earth will disappear, but my words will never disappear. Believe and accept yourself just the way Father sees you, because His words will stand forever. Every other evil shameful labels thrown by the society, family and even few believers in Christ is not the REAL YOU! Trust His word - He calls you bold, beautiful, warrior, mountain mover and unique in your own way because you are his child even after all the fire you've been through. Many didn't finish strong as you.

Congratulate your bravery for passing all your challenges.

Every human is unique and different. You don't have to have the same gifts and qualities of others around you, there's a specific and unique gift within you that makes each and every individual to be different and not the same. It's time to celebrate your personality, character and every inch of your body. Psalms 139:14 - I praise you because I am fearfully and wonderfully made; your works are wonderful, I know that full well. Get comfortable in knowing and believing that you are BEAUTIFUL, every part of your body is beautifully created with a unique skin texture and a priceless structure with your God given height and weight. Every time the word of God hits your heart, learn to own it as it is personally yours and receive it with a joyful heart. So, these lines are specifically designed for you who is reading, allow Holy Spirit to fill you with the love of the LORD JESUS as He's describing you as a beautiful creation. When the world treats you as a curse and an embarrassment, the Lord will name you as wonderful and accept you for the REAL YOU!

Beloved, if God so loved us, we also ought to love one another - 1 John 4:11. Though we are many - parents, ministry leaders, entrepreneurs, sinners and saints, God only sees us as one thing: His Beloved! We might believe we are the beloved of God consciously; may be we hear it all the time. But many of us struggle to truly believe it unconsciously. Celebrate and own this word today. You are His Beloved. LORD JESUS would personally want to connect with his beautiful "Beloved" every second that the breath in the lungs is functioning. The world receives and invites people by appearance, background, status and good reputation which is a very cheap standard of this society, unfortunately this is followed by few of the believers in Christ as well. That is the reality of the world. The rejection of the world is our acceptance in heavenly realms. We are Heaven's Citizen. John 17:16 - They are not of the world, even as I am not of it. Walk away from every atmosphere treating you with no acceptance and get inside your prayer closet. Father loves it when you personally sit in His presence to pour your heart out.

Psalm 56:8 - You keep track of all my sorrows. You have collected all my tears in your bottle. You have recorded each one in your book. The crowd around you might be bored and fed up sometimes with your depression, tears and sorrows but today come to a revelation that someone is waiting for you to pour your tears which is held in His bottle. Even if the ministers and authorities have embarrassed your situation sometimes, just know that Father is still holding account of all your tears shed in His presence. Your tears are not your identity anymore, every drop of tears is turned into pearls for your crown today! Isaiah 62:3 - You shall be a crown of beauty in the hand of the LORD, and a royal diadem in the hand of your God. This is your season and time to know that your battles have refined you in fire and you've passed the test of trials and tribulations. John 6:37 - All those the Father gives me will come to me, and whoever comes to me I will never drive away. God has taken a note of every rejection that you underwent from a very young age and He is a Father who will never reject you. You are in safe hands now as you are reading His word now.

Young David was overlooked and wasn't considered to be anointed, he was the least in the eyes of his own family. But, God saw him and noticed his heart. You might be having such a background where the world has counted you out due to the disasters that took place in your life. But the Lord is encouraging you today through 1 Samuel 16:7 - But the LORD said to Samuel, "Do not consider his appearance or his height, for I have rejected him. The LORD does not look at the things people look. You are the David that God has chosen in your family to accomplish His purposes through your story to the dying world. Don't be discouraged with all the wrong labels put on you, instead rejoice in the hardship that you have endured with the strength of the Lord.

Time to burn every shame, abuse, rejections and loneliness out of your thoughts, emotions and heart with the fire of Holy Spirit. Allow the Holy Spirit to be your best friend from today, He's the comforter right now helping you to discover the real you today. Cherish and Celebrate the Real You in Christ and forget the old identity, for you are new from today. Believe this with all your heart and say out loud the below prayer.

**PRAYER**- Father, I humbly come into your presence with the blood of Jesus all over me, Lord thank you for healing me today with the word of your truth. Help me to carry your precious Holy Spirit throughout my life, help me live a life pleasing and honoring you from today. I know my true identity is in you Lord, thank you for helping me celebrate the Real Me which is in you. Equip me with everything that you have to glorify your name Lord. Hide me in your presence Lord. In Jesus name I pray. Amen.

# 5

# You Are Designed for Greatness

# You Are Designed for Greatness

Shame promotes you for a double portion of blessing. Isaiah 61:7 - Instead of your shame you will receive a double portion, and instead of disgrace you will rejoice in your inheritance. And so you will inherit a double portion in your land, and everlasting joy will be yours. Only if you are bold enough to receive this revelation today, all the miserable moments in your atmosphere will start bringing you the double portion of blessing as written in God's word. Shame qualifies us for a double portion of blessing as per God's word. Joseph went through humiliation, his dreams were only a joke to his own household, Esther was an orphan and she was promoted to be in the palace that made nations to be surrendered, Ruth was a widow and became a real estate owner added to it she was blessed with a wealthy husband, David was the least in the home and yet God anointed him to be the king over Israel, so you see, be in the presence of the Lord no matter what happens around you.

True soldiers are made out of bloodshed and tears, they are the strongest ones God could rely for His purpose to be released on this earth. Romans 8:28 NLT - And we know that God causes everything to work together for the good of those who love God and are called according to his purpose for them. Hence every shame, rejection, abuse, sexual harassment, betrayal, fatherless moments, abandonment, emotional traumas, the unseen tears on your life is a divine plan of the Almighty God to display His greatness through your life, His light is on you.

The God almighty used our Lord Jesus to bring the salvation to the entire world only by suffering, betrayal, shame, insults and pain. Our souls are saved today because of His shame, suffering, insults and pain. Hence in order to be great, bloodshed is required. Congratulations on your journey to greatness as you are eligible for this due to your pain.

It is time for you to walk and talk in the way you are designed to operate. Stop being a people pleaser or you are never going to make your destiny that God has designed for you.

The more you please people it will be hard for your real nature to be revealed and it gives the enemy of your soul the ground to keep you oppressed for a changed fake version of yourself which leads you to be in bondage and the emotions are stuck causing depression and sadness leading to mental illness and pills. It is very important to be yourself to walk a life of greatness. In order to enjoy the blessings that the Father releases on your lives, you need to have a receiving heart and a courageous will power to testify his goodness to the unbelievers without shame. This is one of the major task of greatness you are called for. Boldness is required for the testimony to be uttered out of your mouth. Boldness arises by walking in freedom. Father wants to see you walk free and bold for who you are. Respecting and honouring the elders, leaders, authority is different from pleasing them. You are created to please your creator alone and He is Yahweh who has given His own breath for your existence. It is not humans who give you the license to breathe and walk, it is God! Isaiah 51:12 - "I, yes I, am the one who comforts you. So why are you afraid of mere humans, who wither like the grass and disappear? So, you see, when God has promised a double portion of blessings for the shame and rejections you've been through, no human or demon from hell can stop nor steal the blessings of God on your life. Stop living in fear of humans from today. Dare to enter the life of greatness designed for you. Your blessings are released as you walk in your destiny that God wants to accomplish through your testimony.

Smile and walk like you are entering a palace from now. You are destined to impact the world. You are belonging to the royal bloodline of Lord Jesus Christ. Isaiah 54:4-5 NLT - Fear not; you will no longer live in shame. Don't be afraid; there is no more disgrace for you. You will no longer remember the shame of your youth and the sorrows of widowhood. 5 For your Creator will be your husband; the LORD of Heaven's Armies is his name! He is your Redeemer, the Holy One of Israel, the God of all the earth. You might be a single parent, divorced, abused from childhood, sexually harassed, fatherless and abandoned, bullied with names called out, humiliated for physical appearance, broken home and emotional traumas.

The Lord wants you to live a life with a head held high, not sad and depressed anymore. You are free to be a fearless child of God because of His promise. Shame is no more your portion. Jeremiah 31:3 - The LORD appeared to us in the past, saying: " I have loved you with an everlasting love: I have drawn you with unfailing kindness. Take some time to own this word of everlasting love that is resting upon you. No matter how the world takes you further, God is serious in conveying His genuine love today. Trust His love and take his purposes in your hand without delay. 1 Peter 4:10-11 - Each of you should use whatever gift you have received to serve others, as faithful stewards of God's grace in its various forms. V 11 - If anyone speaks, they should do so as one who speaks the very words of God. If anyone serves, they should do so with the strength God provides, so that in all things God may be praised through Jesus Christ. To him be the glory and the power for ever and ever. Amen. Your greatness is found in your calling. Each and every season of your life has an assignment with His kingdom and there are unique talents and gifts deposited in you for His glory. Start executing it from now, don't wait for anymore confirmation. If you are already serving the Lord, it is time for your promotion in the kingdom. Don't disqualify and shy away yourself this season holding your pasts and pain of shame, refuse to stay there as the Lord wants you to be promoted.

John 15:16 - You did not choose me, but I chose you and appointed you so that you might go and bear fruit, fruit that will last, and so that whatever you ask in my name the Father will give you. You are chosen by Him and not people. You are chosen for greatness by default because of the victories that the Lord has given you from all the attacks of the enemies from your birth. You might be unnoticed, not celebrated, uninvited, not accepted everywhere but here is the Lord welcoming you into His kingdom to work for Him in a greater way. If you have undergone the shame of barrenness for a long time, take courage to receive a miracle any moment soon. Barrenness is not just physical but more spiritual. Psalm 113:9 NIV - He gives the childless woman a FAMILY, making her a happy mother. Praise the LORD! Become pregnant with every dreams and visions that the Lord gives you this season. If the world has shamed you for not conceiving, heaven is rejoicing and welcoming you as a valuable woman and a HAPPY MOTHER by introducing you to a family.

Start exploring the kingdom by serving Lord Jesus with your potentials and release the dream and vision He has placed in your heart and you'll be amazed to hear the word Mother.

If you are battling as a single parent or as a widow, be encouraged today with the favour of God that will come upon your future. Be a Ruth in the field to bring all your gifts and talents to expand His kingdom which will give you favour and a second chance. Psalm 68:6 NLT - God places the lonely in families; he sets the prisoners free and gives them joy. But he makes the rebellious live in a sun-scorched land. Every rejections in the world is the acceptance in the Heaven. Your pasts, mistakes, sin, abusive childhood or anything that has tormented your life is not your true identity. You are the Child of a Righteous King who sits in the right hand of the Father, by interceding and expecting your arrival for Kingdom roles. Everything that belongs to the king belongs to you as well. Your true home is heaven and this earth is a passing cloud. You are a moving passenger to reach your destiny which is high and above.

The Lord counts you as Precious and His very Own. He wants you be filled with peace and joy. This can be made possible only with an intimate relationship with Him through Holy Spirit. It's interesting to build this connection with the LORD by inviting the Precious Holy Spirit given to every believing hearts as a free gift. Holy Spirit is an amazing friend and strength, He's a person bubbling with joy to empower you with the intimacy of the LORD. (Read Ephesians 1:13). Have a believing Heart, a believer who dares the heart to completely believe can break barriers and reach heights unimaginable.

Are you ready to walk in greatness orchestrated by the Father? Then get ready to re-surrender your life to Lord Jesus once again. He rejects nobody returning to Him in search of affection and love. Though He is God, He understands each and every pain that you have faced as a human. Plant yourself in a local church and start serving Him with all capacities, search Him in your personal prayer closet everyday. Jeremiah 29:13 NLT - If you look for me wholeheartedly, you will find me. Opening your heart and pouring your tears during pain is a form of worship unto Him, start doing it instead of reaching humans for sharing your pain.

The response from the crowd will not always satisfy and it might hurt you sometimes. So get connected with the Holy Spirit in tough times and you'll find your destiny. As you start giving your personal space to Jesus and as your gifts and talents are given as a service to His kingdom, the Heaven will start answering all your prayers. I am the living testimony on that. When everybody left me and judged on my situation, God lifted me and answered my prayers. Don't deny the calling on your life due to the circumstances, instead, rest on each and every promise to be fully manifested through your life. God wants to see a Joseph, Esther, David, Ruth, Daniel, Deborah, Peter, Paul in you, He wants His glory to be revealed through every dark situation of your life. Isaiah 60:1 NIV - Arise, Shine, for your light has come, and the glory of the LORD rises upon you. It's time for you to rise from the ashes and show the world the light that God has filled for His glory. Execute every dreams and visions that the Lord has given from now. Be bold to walk in the true freedom that God has given in His identity. You are a New Person now!

**PRAYER-** Father I come into your presence with the blood of Jesus today. I thank you for accepting me as your own child. I bless your name for redeeming me from all my sins with your blood Lord. I receive the gift of grace and salvation given for my soul through your blood Lord. May your name be glorified greatly through my life Lord, fill me up with the precious Holy Spirit to live a life of surrender. Lord I commit my soul, spirit and body into your mighty hands. May your power be seen in my life to complete everything that you've called me for, May you stir up my gifts and talents for your glory. Help me have an excellent spirit as I start serving you wherever you place me. May everything that I do please you and may the kingdom of God be established here on earth. In Jesus name I pray Amen.

# 6

# Dare To Break the Stereotype

# Dare To Break the Stereotype

John 4:7-10 NLT - Soon a Samaritan woman came to draw water, and Jesus said to her, "Please give me a drink." [8] He was alone at the time because his disciples had gone into the village to buy some food. [9] The woman was surprised, for Jews refuse to have anything to do with Samaritans. She said to Jesus, "You are a Jew, and I am a Samaritan woman. Why are you asking me for a drink?" [10] Jesus replied, "If you only knew the gift God has for you and who you are speaking to, you would ask me, and I would give you living water.

The woman who had 5 husbands was qualified to be standing next to Lord Jesus. How many times have you allowed your circumstances to disqualify yourself from receiving His closeness to you? This gives us a revelation of God seeing every single soul on this planet with the righteousness of Jesus over us. When we believe His death on the cross and accept Him as our Lord and Saviour, He draws closer to our life, purpose and destiny by breaking every religion and culture! The society, family, friends or even the believers in church might judge our ways and sins, but this kind of life draws Him closer to us only to convict and destroy the power of hell stealing our future and destiny.

He never condemns but convicts to stop sinning and to draw us closer to the great life meant to live in eternity. The woman replied with all insecurities that was flooding in her heart as Jews have no business with the samaritans. Just like that woman, you might be wondering if such a Holy God the Father is really speaking to you and getting closer to you. Yes, He is right now and this is the hour He is really pursuing you, without doubt believe it. There is something within you that He wants you to accomplish for establishing a testimony unto His name to reach the dying and the hurting world out there. The Samaritan woman was not only chosen to stand beside Jesus but He asked for a drink. The very drink that He is asking you today is your time, focus, attention and your investment towards His kingdom from now. For God to accomplish His plans and purposes on earth it only requires FAITH, not our past histories. Would you dare to have that FAITH for breaking the religious lies spoken against your life by taking Jesus by your side today?

V10 Jesus replied, "If you only knew the gift God has for you and who you are speaking to, you would ask me, and I would give you living water.

The moment you start believing about hearing the voice of Jesus around you, your heart will automatically become courageous and it will dare to ask more of water that the Lord wants to offer over your life specifically. It's not for everyone, this opportunity doesn't knock everybody's door, you know why? Because everyone doesn't believe. Which means the Lord wants to move in your life as He has seen that faith in you.

Joshua 1:9 NIV - Have I not commanded you, Be strong and courageous. Do not be afraid; do not be discouraged, for the Lord your God will be with you wherever you go. There's a demand on your life to be bold and courageous. This book hasn't reached you by accident. The Lord orchestrates each and every detail of your life well in advance, and this is the exact kairos moment for you and your future. Be brave to believe and stir up your faith now to hear the Fathers heart and His promises towards your life.

Isaiah 43:18,19 NIV - Forget the former things; do not dwell on the past. See, I am doing a new thing! Now it springs up; do you not perceive it? I am making a way in the wilderness and streams in the wasteland.

This word brings you a confirmation that your past is falling to the ground today, your new beginning starts from this moment as you start believing the word of the Lord.

Every other voices that speaks shame and insults are from the enemy and they have no power over you. Dare to believe the Lord to do a new thing in your life and He will honor your faith for releasing His supernatural miracles towards your destiny. Don't encourage the sound of Pharisees in your mind and heart, the Lord knows and He can move through your life. Focus on Jesus alone. When He commands, the river is birthed out of desert, the waves and storms in your life will be silenced at His voice for His voice is lightning and thunder. It can break and burn all your strongholds at the shout of His name. The Lord is finding the uniqueness in you to make the impossible happen. Stop believing the religious lies and enter into your destiny and purpose with boldness.

Ignore the negativity around your life that you've heard so long, it might be in your closest circle too. When God finds your faith worthy, nobody can stop His purpose from happening.

Heaven and earth responds when God appoints a person on an assignment aligned with the will of God. Because you carry the spirit of Joshua, God wants you to break the stereotype for the current generation.

Judges 5:7 - Villagers in Israel would not fight; they held back until I, Deborah, arose, until I arose, a mother in Israel. The Lords sees you as a pioneer in faith for a lot many reasons. The courage and battles that you've endured as a child is noticed by the heaven. There were situations in your life, where you were overlooked, unappreciated, unrecognized and humiliated for having a kind heart. But the Almighty Father has taken notice of your kindness, the pure heart that you carry is highly valued by Abba in heaven. You can be the lamp for your bloodline, the pain and trauma that has crossed over your life has made you a true warrior in the spiritual realm. You are capable leader in the sight of the Lord for never giving up your faith so far. Congratulations!

Believe and release your faith by praying the below prayer aloud, for you were born for such a time as this. (Read Esther 4:14)

**PRAYER -** Father, I come into your presence with a humble heart today. Thank you for speaking and affirming your word unto me Lord. You are worthy to be worshipped and praised Lord. Forgive me for not understanding your voice. I surrender my life to you from this day Lord, use it for your purpose and your glory Lord. May your kingdom come and your will be done through me Lord. In Jesus name I pray Amen.

# 7

## You Are Not A Burden

# You Are Not a Burden

His very own hands takes care of the needy. It gives Him pleasure and joy to feed the homeless, fatherless and orphans. Psalms 10:17, 18 - You, LORD, hear the desire of the afflicted; you encourage them, and you listen to their cry, Defending the fatherless and the oppressed, so that mere earthly mortals will never again strike terror. God has always blessed me with encouragement. The people around would discount me and never consider me for appreciation due to my background and social status, but the Sovereign God has always counted my feelings and tears. He never saw me the way the world saw. Similarly, if you are wondering why your life was full of discouragement, it is time for you to know that the enemy Has lied to you as you are a burden with nobody to look after. That is the biggest lie for you to cut off right away. The fact is, you are loved, you are cherished, you are a blessing as you belong to the Most High God. Every secret tears in your bed is noticed by your father. He is coming with an appreciation for everything that you have endured. He wants to have a personal relationship with you like never before. He wants to re-introduce you to the world in a brighter and the best version of yourself. Would you believe Him for that?

Your situation is not a surprise to God, He is your creator and He wants you reach your destiny and you are not a burden! Nehemiah 4:14 – Don't be afraid of them. Remember the Lord, who is great and awesome, and fight for your families, your sons and your daughters, your wives and your homes.

Our God is an almighty who battles for our families; spouse and children, there are one million ways for God to provide for you and your family, His hand is never shortened to help you, His arms are capable of lifting your heavy loads that were wrongly placed in your life by the enemy all these years. We as His children are fed and protected as per the Government of Heaven and not by the economy of this physical world. As per the world, the needs of our life might seem to be a burden in our natural eyes. He wants us have the supernatural eyes of faith to see Him and trust His word of hope for the manifestation of the true riches of His kingdom. Every need of your life will be met by Jesus. The eyes that seek Him will never be put to shame; He is a head lifter and a promoter. He is a shield to those that trust Him. Your story is about to change and you are marked by Heaven for His glory.

Psalms 30:5 Tears may flow in the night, but joy comes in the morning. The Lord is concerned and has noticed the tears that have fallen out of your eyes for the false accusations, labels of the society, cheap names given by fake friends, family members and sometimes even believers in the church. He knows your past and yet does not judge you. He wants your heart to be healed completely. Jeremiah 30:17 – But I will restore you to health and heal your wounds, declares the Lord, because you are called an outcast, Zion for whom no one cares. You are not a mistake. Allow the Lord to heal the bleeding scars within your heart by believing this word. You were made for a purpose and that is to worship Him. As you start worshiping the Lord with a complete surrender, your true identity will be revealed. All the other labels that followed you these many years is coming to an end in Jesus name. Walk in the authority and power given by your heavenly Father.

Keep your head high as you start walking from now. God honours your faith when it is impossible to trust Him, trust Him anyway. Even with little faith He can perform wonders in your life.

He is the owner of every species on this Universe and He has power to change your story in a second. He is the owner of times and season. He sees something special and unique in you which the world has ignored. Our God is excellent in noticing the rejected things of this world. You are a treasure in His sight being noticed always. Psalms 33:13, 14 – From heaven the LORD looks down and sees all mankind. From his dwelling place He watches all who live on the earth. So you see, every bit of your life has never gone unnoticed. Your father in heaven appreciates your bravery and courage for facing all the odds and challenges of life that you have taken. He sees you as a champion and an absolute over comer not a burden at all. You might have never received any appreciation or recognition for your brave qualities, but the Lord from heaven sees you and recognizes you. There are rewards waiting on your name. Hebrews 11:6- And without faith it is impossible to please God, because anyone who comes to him must believe that he exists and that he rewards those who earnestly seek him. This word is for you, receive with faith.

Every moment which your heart searched Him even with doubts in your mind, He has taken notice of it. And there are rewards for every minute that you showed your faith in searching Him. You are close to stepping into your calling and into your purpose which is designed by your creator Abba. It takes your surrender and faith to see the bigger picture of God's glory revealing through your life. Through your obedience the upcoming generation can search God with spirit and truth by seeing you following Him with passion.

Ecclesiastes 1:9 there is nothing new under the sun. The Lord knows the deepest desire in your heart and He longs to visit you. Everything that stands as an obstacle or a huge wall for you is nothing in His sight. Open up your heart to give your heaviness to Him. Mathew 11:28 Come to me, all you who are weary and burdened, and I will give you rest. God is inviting you to surrender everything that bothers you to Him today. Trust His word and start surrendering your concerns to Him. Psalms 62:8 - Trust in him at all times, you people; pour out your hearts to him, for God is our refuge. Literally, at all times means every breath of your life. Trust God's words and rebuke the lies out of your head. God can make a way where there is no way.

He is specialist in creating a new one! If you've been haunted so long with negative voices around you, today it comes to an end in the mighty name of Jesus! Believe it. You are not a burden but a child of Most High. Keep declaring this over your life. Past traumas have no more room in your life anymore. God is breathing His Ruach (breath) over you as you read these lines right away as you have faith in His word. You are healed, made new and restored for a new beginning from this day. Nothing from your past shall touch you nor have power over your life in Jesus mighty name.

Every lies that were spoken to you all these years is falling to the ground now as you believe in the name of Jesus. You are healed and made new completely. Isaiah 43:18 – Remember ye not the former things, neither consider the things of old. Behold, I will do a new thing; now it shall spring forth; shall ye not know it? I will even make a way in the wilderness, and rivers in the desert. Any negative voice that discourages you as this life is difficult and hopeless is a demonic lie. These lies will not prosper anymore. You are born for the glory of the Father in heaven, He allowed shame and rejection in your life, only to decorate and crown your life for His glory.

Isaiah 54:7 – For a brief moment I abandoned you, but with great compassion I will gather you. Every rejection in your life falls to the ground now in Jesus name. Allow the Holy Spirit to minister you by this word. Walk with this confirmation that your life will no longer be in circles but upright for the hand of the Lord is upon you from now. His compassion is flooded towards you in every step of your life. You are not alone in this Journey. A mighty God is guarding and zealously walking along with you. God sees you as an end time revivalist, your testimony matters to the world. There are lives attached towards your purpose. 2 Corinthians 5:7 We walk by faith and not by sight. Start seeing through the eyes of faith from today.

Have faith and give your complete life to Jesus by praying the below prayer aloud.

**PRAYER -** Heavenly Father, I come into your presence with praises and thanksgiving Lord. Forgive all my sins and I repent all my disobedience towards your voice. Thank you for speaking to me today, I praise you Lord for letting me know that I am not a burden anymore but a Victorious child in your kingdom. Here I am to surrender my everything. May your glory be full of this earth and May your purposes come alive In Jesus name.

I would like to thank you for investing in this book. May the the physical manifestation of every promise that you received from this book begin to manifest in Jesus Name. You are not cursed but blessed, you are not fatherless but a Heavenly Father in high places owns you, You are not a widow and separated person but there's a Husband admiring you from heaven, You are not barren but a happy Mother in an everlasting kingdom, You are not homeless but a child of the Most High seated in heavenly realms, the battles and shame of your life has qualified you to be the royal priesthood for an eternal kingdom. May this empower you to take up the assignments released by the Lord in your secret place. May God crown His glory upon you and May His presence rest upon you everywhere you go. The Lord has crowned you with His glory.

**Isaiah 62:3 NLT** - The **LORD** will hold you in his hand for all to see—**a splendid crown** in the hand of God. May the **CROWN** out of your **SHAME** be a shining light to the world. Own this word of truth and write it in your heart, seal it with His blood. God has covered your shame with the heavenly **CROWN**. Start wearing it and enjoy every step of your life from now.

**TO DO LIST** - I challenge you to write down your God given vision today without wasting a second. Habakkuk 2:2 KJV - And the LORD answered me, and said, Write the vision, and make it plain upon tables, that he may run that readeth it.

You have a purpose to be fulfilled. Write down the big dreams and visions that you want from God to be fulfilled. He will help you accomplish it at the right time and the right season. You are ordained and anointed for everything that the Lord has called you far. May the Holy Spirit empower you to step into God's calling now. God bless you for the time spent and May you grow and expand in His kingdom.

## ANOINTING - Isaiah 10:27 NLT

In that day the LORD will end the bondage of his people. He will break the yoke of slavery and lift it from their shoulders.

Yeshua hamashiach is your anointed King Anointing you now with His word, Truth and Power. You are released from your old life to step into a new version in Christ this day. Every yokes and burdens that enslaved you all these years is broken now with the power of His anointing. Be released to your true destiny.

Your are chosen, called and anointed with His Spirit. Be washed with the blood of Jesus as your soul is getting transformed now with His Divinely order. You will no more walk in confusion but with clarity.

## Isaiah 30:21 NLT

Your own ears will hear him. Right behind you a voice will say, "This is the way you should go," whether to the right or to the left.

Congratulations on your new path, for your God ordained season has begun now. Walk with authority and power as a true child of God and you will never be in shame again in the name of Jesus.

# Enjoy Your Crown

# About Our Ministry

Pastor Rahul and I are the founders of Love Came Down Ministries. From the beginning, we have had the vision to raise nations with Praise & worship and to take the gospel to the broken and the rejected. My husband has poured into teenagers as a Pastor, teacher of Discipleship trainings and school of Worship across globe and God has used him in Countries like Kenya, Uganda, Indonesia, Malaysia, Nepal, Sri- lanka, borders of Philippines and India. Rahul holds a BTh from Charis university India. He became a associate pastor at the age of 21 in B2B Coimbatore, and for 4 years he travelled across the globe as a pastor. In 2016 at the age of 26, He acquired Doctorate of Ministry - Affiliated by AACT - USA, Accredited by WWAC - USA. For 3 years, He was a lead pastor for the Tamil congregation in Destiny C3 India, Bangalore. In 2023 October at the age of 30, soon after our marriage we were led by the Lord to Pioneer the vision that God placed in our hearts.

Rahul's journey began in India, where he was born into a devout Hindu household. He got saved at the age of 12 from a deadly brain fever. His calling manifested early when he took on the role of a Worship leader at just 14 years of age. His dynamic style and deep understanding of Scripture along with keen knowledge of music in various language quickly made him a sought-after speaker and worship leader at various conferences and Christian gatherings across globe. The spiritual warfare was so heavy resulting in the failure of previous marriage. It was during this waiting season we met each other and decided to accept each other in marriage to serve the Lord in full capacity.

We long to see the full manifestation of the potentials that the Lord has kept on each and every failed marriage, broken homes and families to come alive for the Lord's glory. The enemy wants the families to be killed so that their God given destinies can be aborted, but here we are a living testimony to support and bring them in teaching and training to fight the battles with Christ.

We are dedicated to soul-winning, healing, deliverance, and the raising up of young leaders. In addition to pastoring, we extend our ministry through the worship, mission and revival movement and digital media, YouTube channel. We would like to offer Worship E - Courses through our online learning platform, through the online school making theology and Christian living accessible to a global audience.

# Special Thanks-

Taking a small moment to thank my Husband who encouraged, supported and helped in every step of this book. I thank the Almighty Father for blessing me with an absolute amazing partner who understands the kingdom goals of a woman. My heartfelt gratitude to Rahul for being an absolute blessing in the journey of this assignment.

**IN THE RIGHT HANDS, THIS BOOK WILL CHANGE LIVES-**

Most of the people who need this message will not be looking for this book. To change their lives, you need to put a copy of this book in their hands.

**Matthew 13:8 NLT**

Still other seeds fell on fertile soil, and they produced a crop that was thirty, sixty, and even a hundred times as much as had been planted!

Our ministry is constantly seeking methods to find the good ground, the people who need this timely revelation to change their lives forever. Will you help us reach these people?

**2 Corinthians 9:6 NLT**

Remember this-a farmer who plants only a few seeds will get a small crop. But the one who plants generously will get a generous crop.

EXTEND THIS MINISTRY BY SOWING

BUY 3 BOOKS, 5 BOOKS, 10 BOOKS, OR MORE TODAY, AND BECOME A LFE CHANGER!

FOLLOW US IN ALL OUR SOCIAL MEDIA PAGES GIVEN IN THE BOTTOM OF THIS PAGE BY SUBSCRIBING LIKING SHARING AND COMMENTING ON ALL OUR PAGES.

THANK YOU!

Share your testimony if this book has transformed your mind and life. Write to us your prayer requests to the below email id.

Email:  info@lcdglobal.org

Website:  www.lcdglobal.org

IG - @lcdglobal  IG - @kani.david

IG - @rahulprabhuj

www.ingramcontent.com/pod-product-compliance
Lightning Source LLC
LaVergne TN
LVHW061622070526
838199LV00078B/7394